I See Insects

Bee

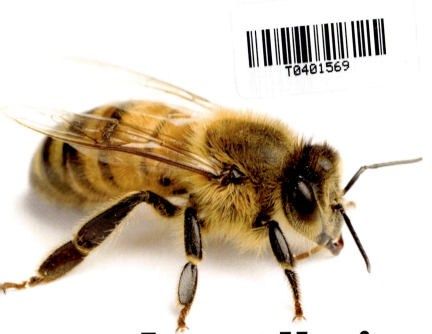

written by August Hoeft

Xist Publishing
INSPIRING DISCOVERY & DELIGHT

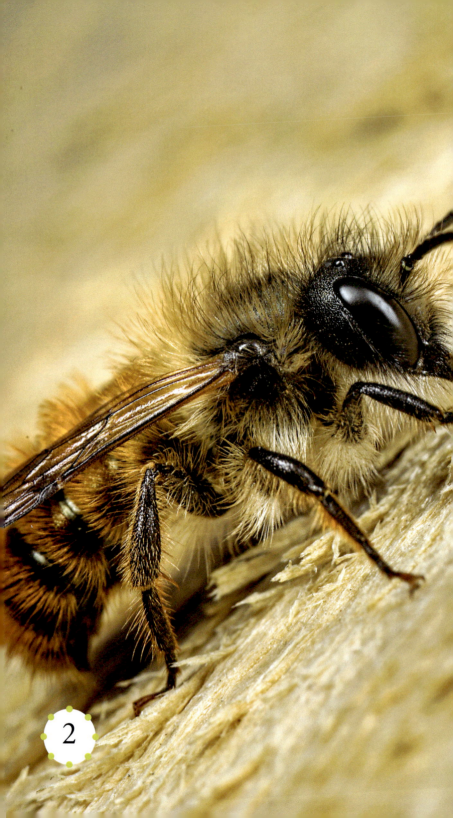

I see a bee.

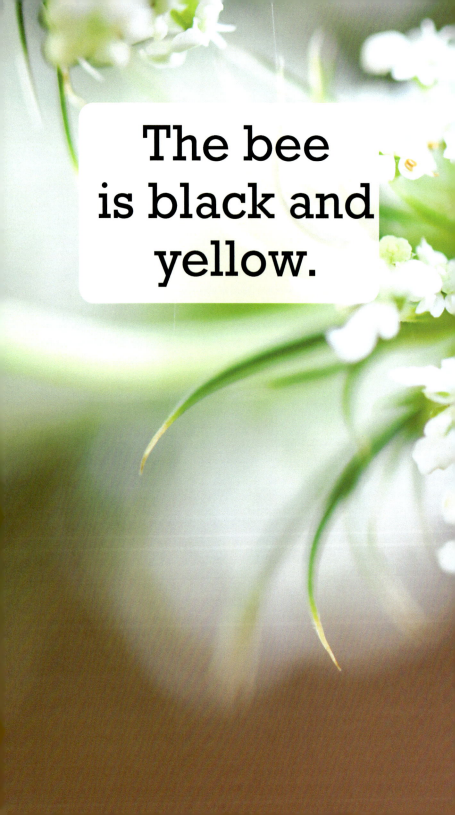
The bee is black and yellow.

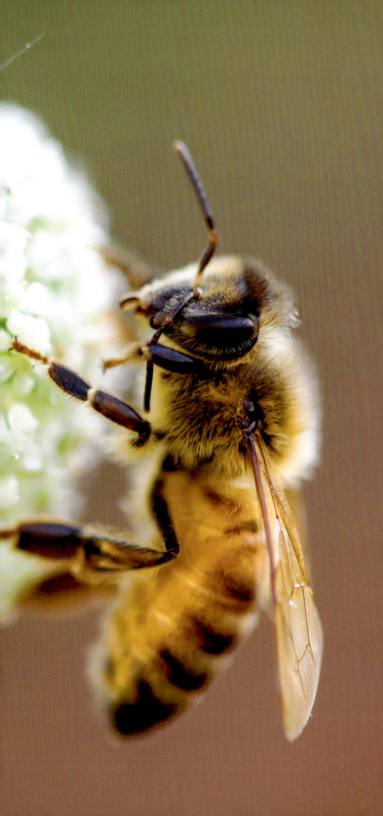

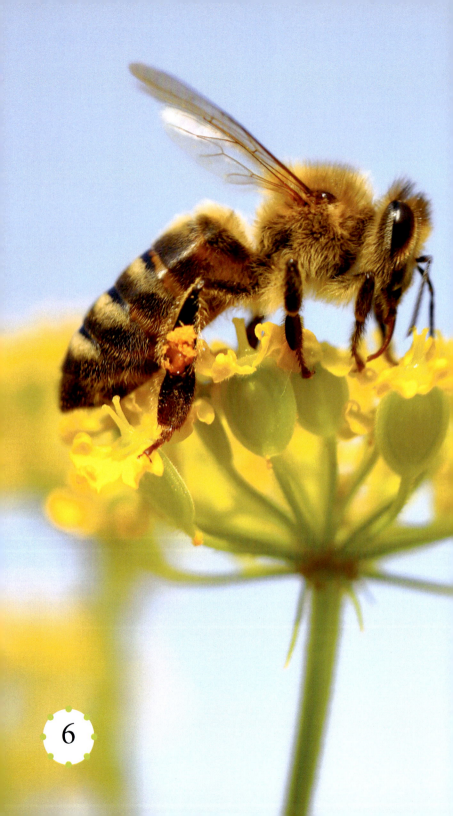

The bee has wings.

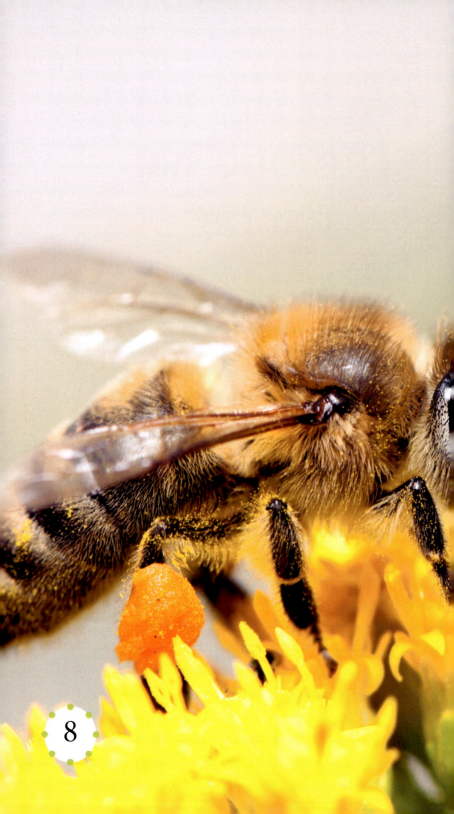

The bee collects pollen.

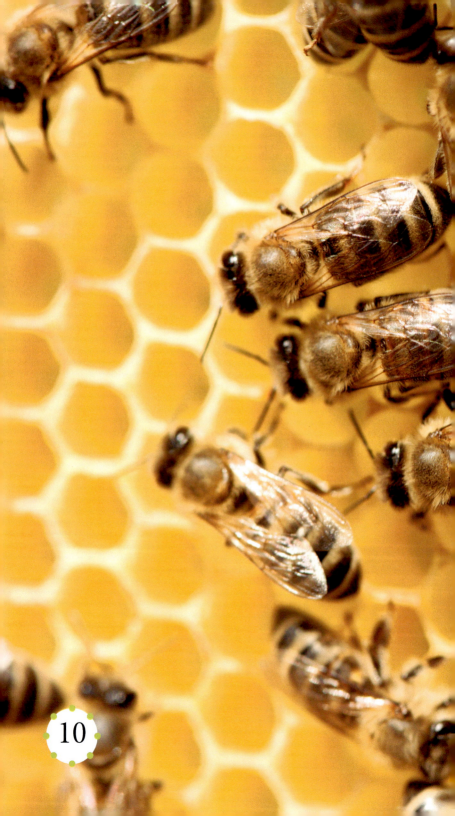

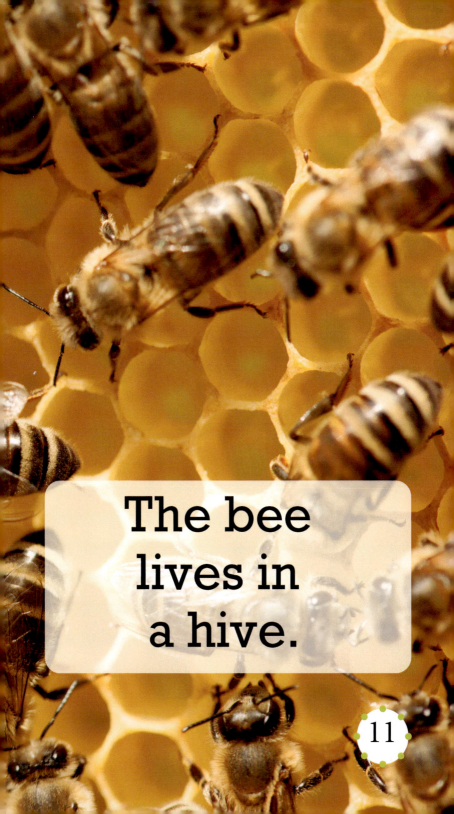

The bee lives in a hive.

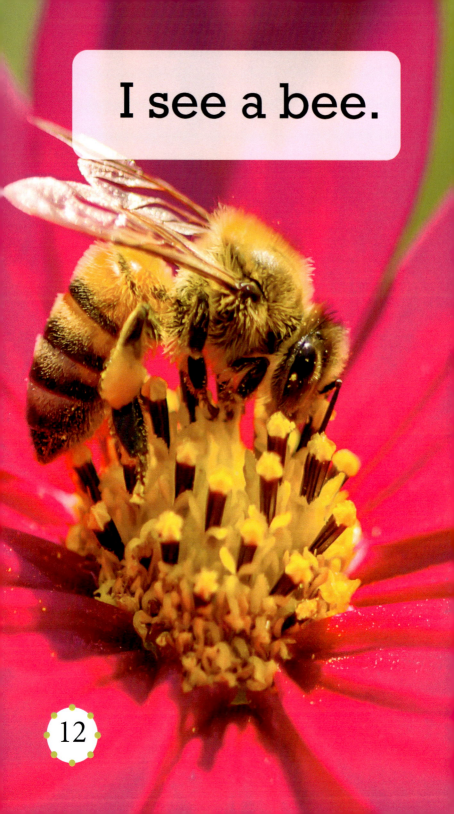

I see a bee.

12